MW00476267

DAILY
AFFIRMATIONS
for

Healing

Love After Heartbreak, Vol. I
COMPANION BOOK

STEPHAN LABOSSIERE
@stephanspeaks

Daily Affirmations for Healing
Love After Heartbreak, Vol. 1 Companion Book

Copyright ©2019 by Stephan Labossiere for Stephan Speaks, LLC
Published by Highly Favored Publishing
First Edition: September 2019

All rights reserved. No part of this book may be used or reproduced in any manner whatsoever without written permission except in the case of brief quotations embodied in critical articles or reviews.

For information, contact Highly Favored Publishing –
highlyfavoredent@gmail.com

Unless otherwise indicated, all Scripture quotations are taken from the Holy Bible, New Living Translation, copyright © 1996, 2004, 2015 by Tyndale House Foundation. Used by permission of Tyndale House Publishers, Inc., Carol Stream, Illinois 60188. All rights reserved.

Scripture quotations marked (NIV) are taken from the Holy Bible, New International Version®, NIV®. Copyright © 1973, 1978, 1984, 2011 by Biblica, Inc.™ Used by permission of Zondervan. All rights reserved worldwide. www.zondervan.com The "NIV" and "New International Version" are trademarks registered in the United States Patent and Trademark Office by Biblica, Inc.™

Editor & Creative Consultant: C. Nzingha Smith

Formatting: Ya Ya Ya Creative – www.yayayacreative.com

ISBN No. 978-0-9980189-8-0

PRINTED AND BOUND IN THE UNITED STATES OF AMERICA

Table of Contents

Table of Contents

Introduction

———⟨⟩———

Daily Affirmations for Healing is a companion book for *Love After Heartbreak, Vol I*. The purpose of this book is to provide you with a daily tool you can use to further strengthen the results of your self-healing journey.

Why affirmations? According to Psychology Today, "Generally speaking, affirmations are used to reprogram the subconscious mind, to encourage us to believe certain things about ourselves or about the world and our place within it. They are also used to help us create the reality we want—often in terms of making (or attracting) wealth, love, beauty, and happiness."

What you believe about yourself and the results that you've had in life thus far can both be traced back to the things that you say about yourself and what you believe to be true for you.

Your reality is a result of what you think. In order to change what you think, you need to be intentional about what it is you're saying to yourself on a consistent basis.

Positive affirmations work twofold. They help you to reprogram your mind and subconscious mind as well as help you to feel empowered and better about yourself in real time. The key to reaping the benefits of affirmations is repetition.

I wrote this book to simply help you affirm some of the things that we've already worked through in *Love After Heartbreak, Vol. I* as well as in the *Healing Heartbreak Journal*. I want you to get the most out of your hard work. Simply reading through the material is not going to get you the results you desire. You need to really use all of these resources in an ongoing manner for complete transformation.

I've focused the affirmations around different areas we've spent a lot of time covering in the above-mentioned books. Mind, body, emotions, spirituality, finances, and relationships. In addition to the positive affirmations, I've also included a release affirmation.

Anytime we look to replace something, we need to get rid of or release that which doesn't work before we try to replace it with another (better) option.

To help ground you, I've also included a scripture study and a daily prayer. These two additions are to help you to understand that lasting change and transformation require God's help. There is only so much you can do on your own. You need God and the great news is that God wants to help you be the person He created you to be.

Also, instead of overwhelming you with a ton of different affirmations to memorize and try to incorporate into your daily life. I have focused in on seven powerful affirmations for each category. One for every day of the week. You will read each one for seven days and write a brief reflection at the end of the week. You will then repeat the group of seven for a total of 5 weeks to help you really get results and see lasting change in your life.

Studies show that it takes an average of 21 days to change a habit. Normally, studies focus on physical habits, but I also believe this to be true where our thought patterns are concerned.

It won't help you to read through them once and expect to see any kind of real change. It's likely that you won't even remember them after the first seven days. However, staying with the same group of focused affirmations over the course of the month will help you to really begin to get out of them what you need.

Some will scream at you louder than others as you work with them and repeat them aloud. This is where the magic happens. You don't have to believe in what you're saying for it to make a difference. To start, it might seem silly or stupid. However, do it anyway.

What do you have to lose? Nothing.

Each group of affirmations includes space for five weekly reflections to help you observe any changes you feel or see in your life. Once you've repeated each group for five weeks, move on to the next focused group.

I encourage you to use your affirmations daily. It won't take you more than five minutes to read a day and fifteen minutes if you're at day seven and need to write a weekly reflection.

You're worth the time and effort.

As always, be open to the information I'm going to share with you. Be willing to do your part. Believe you'll be able to reap the many benefits awaiting you at the end of this journey and it will be possible for you.

Another thing I want to point out is that many of the affirmations begin with "I am."

"I am" is a biblical term for a statement of existence. It came from the Hebrew verb "to be or to exist."

With this statement, God declared that He is self-existent, eternal, self-sufficient, self-directed, and unchanging.

God lives in you. The Spirit of God lives within you. Understand that you are putting God first in the situation by declaring His name and combining it with your present, in-process state, as well as also declaring in advance the finished work.

Know that God loves you.

As you continue on your healing journey with daily affirmations, you're going to really begin to live out the inner work you've done.

You'll be incorporating the changes into your daily lifestyle and habits. However, it will take your making a commitment and sticking to that commitment to experience total transformation inside and out.

Get excited! The very best is in store for you as you use these powerful tools to activate and call forth lasting change in your life.

"The tongue has the power of life and death, and those who love it will eat its fruit."
–Proverbs 18:21, NIV

How To Get the Most Out of Your Daily Affirmations

As often as possible, say each affirmation aloud while looking into a mirror and into your eyes.

For added support you can put your hand on your heart or on your stomach while saying them.

Choose a time of day. Morning, lunch, or at night. Do what works best for you but be consistent.

<u>STEP ONE</u>

Say the "Release Affirmation" out loud at least once. You might need to repeat it before moving on.

Pay attention to how your body reacts from the statement or if you feel any negative emotions. Don't dismiss them or judge them, just pay attention and observe yourself to see what happens.

STEP TWO

Ground yourself in the daily "Positive Affirmation." Smile while saying it aloud. Allow the positive energy to melt away any previous feelings of dis-ease. Be thankful for the change taking place in that moment.

STEP THREE

Take time to read and recite the daily "Scripture Study" aloud to further solidify God's word and promises for your life. A big block in manifesting the life God has for you is that you don't know who you are in God. Aligning with God's word will help unlock favor and blessings.

STEP FOUR

Pray the "Daily Prayer" once aloud and once silently to yourself. Why is this so important? Because God told us to ask and we shall receive. Seal your affirmation in prayer, which further activates God's power in your life.

<u>STEP FIVE</u>

Sit in silence for a few moments before going about the rest of your day or before you prepare to go to sleep at night, depending on the time you chose.

Again, whatever routine you choose, stick to it.

Prayer

Pray this prayer with me:

Heavenly Father, I pray a release of your supernatural comfort, peace, and grace upon everyone reading this book right now. I pray that you would cleanse us with your healing power and love. Rid us of all the memories from hurt, pain, and disappointment we've endured, which were necessary for our growth and promotion.

God, grant us the gift of patience and determination as we diligently work to implement the changes that we want to see in our lives. I pray that you give us clarity of mind. Open up our eyes of understanding so that we may master the lessons needed to receive, pursue, and recover everything meant for us.

Thank you, God, for renewed faith and courage to do what it takes to be our best selves as you've purposed us to be. We're making the choice to live our lives more abundantly. We're making the decision to co-create the lives we want to live now and going forward according to your will. Your word says, "when two or more are gathered together in your name that you are with them."

Thank you for your presence as we continue our collective healing journeys. By faith, we declare it done and so. Amen.

PART I

Healing
YOUR
Mind AND
Thoughts

Day One

RELEASE AFFIRMATION

I release the need to dwell on the past. The past
only exists in my mind. It's no longer my reality.

POSITIVE AFFIRMATION

I am focusing on being present,
which allows me to experience more
happiness and joy in my life today.

SCRIPTURE STUDY

"Forget the former things, do not dwell on the past."
–Isaiah 43:18, NIV

DAILY PRAYER

God, thank you for giving me the tools to change,
renew, and purify my thoughts and mind. Show
me your vision for my life. Align me to higher
consciousness. I'm done with the repetitive cycles
I've dwelled in, which were caused by old thought
patterns. All things new! It is done and so, Amen.

RELEASE AFFIRMATION

I release the need to think I have to "know-it-all."

POSITIVE AFFIRMATION

I am open to learning and growing in wisdom,
understanding, and knowledge.

SCRIPTURE STUDY

*"Don't turn your back on wisdom, for she will
protect you. Love her and she will guard you."*
–Proverbs 4:6, NLT

DAILY PRAYER

God, thank you for giving me the tools to change,
renew, and purify my thoughts and mind. Show
me your vision for my life. Align me to higher
consciousness. I'm done with the repetitive cycles
I've dwelled in, which were caused by old thought
patterns. All things new! It is done and so, Amen.

Day Three

RELEASE AFFIRMATION

I release the need to be "right" all the time.

POSITIVE AFFIRMATION

I now listen to understand and choose harmony,
love, and happiness over ego.

SCRIPTURE STUDY

*"Above all else clothe yourselves with love, which
binds us all together in perfect harmony."*
–Colossians 3:14, NLT

DAILY PRAYER

God, thank you for giving me the tools to change,
renew, and purify my thoughts and mind. Show
me your vision for my life. Align me to higher
consciousness. I'm done with the repetitive cycles
I've dwelled in, which were caused by old thought
patterns. All things new! It is done and so, Amen.

Day Four

RELEASE AFFIRMATION

I release the need to punish myself with guilt or shame around decisions I've made in the past.

POSITIVE AFFIRMATION

I accept that all of life is an experiment. I am always learning, growing, and improving.

SCRIPTURE STUDY

"…God causes everything to work together for the good of those who love God and are called according to his purpose."
–Romans 8:28, NLT

DAILY PRAYER

God, thank you for giving me the tools to change, renew, and purify my thoughts and mind. Show me your vision for my life. Align me to higher consciousness. I'm done with the repetitive cycles I've dwelled in, which were caused by old thought patterns. All things new! It is done and so, Amen.

Day Five

RELEASE AFFIRMATION

I release the need to create chaos and
drama in my mind and in my life.

POSITIVE AFFIRMATION

I am in control of my thoughts. My thoughts create
my reality and experiences. I will actively think
positively so I can actually experience the positive.

SCRIPTURE STUDY

"Fix your thoughts on what is true, honorable,
right, pure, lovely, admirable. Think about things
that are excellent and praiseworthy."
–Philippians 4:8, NLT

DAILY PRAYER

God, thank you for giving me the tools to change,
renew, and purify my thoughts and mind. Show
me your vision for my life. Align me to higher
consciousness. I'm done with the repetitive cycles
I've dwelled in, which were caused by old thought
patterns. All things new! It is done and so, Amen.

Day Six

RELEASE AFFIRMATION

I release the need to think negatively about myself.

POSITIVE AFFIRMATION

I love, accept, and appreciate myself as I am.

SCRIPTURE STUDY

"So, God created mankind in his own image,
in the image of God he created them..."
–Genesis 1:27, NLT

DAILY PRAYER

God, thank you for giving me the tools to change, renew, and purify my thoughts and mind. Show me your vision for my life. Align me to higher consciousness. I'm done with the repetitive cycles I've dwelled in, which were caused by old thought patterns. All things new! It is done and so, Amen.

Day Seven

RELEASE AFFIRMATION

I release old mindsets and negative
thought patterns.

POSITIVE AFFIRMATION

I am actively choosing to renew my mind
and upgrade my thoughts daily.

SCRIPTURE STUDY

*"Don't copy the behavior and customs of this
world, but let God transform you into a new
person by changing the way you think."*
–Romans 12:2, NLT

DAILY PRAYER

God, thank you for giving me the tools to change,
renew, and purify my thoughts and mind. Show
me your vision for my life. Align me to higher
consciousness. I'm done with the repetitive cycles
I've dwelled in, which were caused by old thought
patterns. All things new! It is done and so, Amen.

Week One Reflection

_____

_____

_____

_____

_____

_____

_____

_____

_____

_____

_____

_____

_____

_____

_____

_____

_____

Week Two Reflection

_____

_____

_____

_____

_____

_____

_____

_____

_____

_____

_____

_____

_____

_____

_____

_____

Week Three Reflection

_____

_____

_____

_____

_____

_____

_____

_____

_____

_____

_____

_____

_____

_____

_____

_____

_____

_____

Week Four Reflection

Week Five Reflection

_____

_____

_____

_____

_____

_____

_____

_____

_____

_____

_____

_____

_____

_____

_____

_____

_____

_____

_____

PART II

Healing

YOUR

Emotions

Day One

RELEASE AFFIRMATION

I release the need to dismiss or lie
about my true feelings.

POSITIVE AFFIRMATION

I matter. My feelings matter. My voice matters.

SCRIPTURE STUDY

*"No more lies, no more pretense…When you lie to
others, you end up lying to yourself."*
–Ephesians 4:25

DAILY PRAYER

God, thank you for this time of growth and healing.
Help me to have the same compassion and
forgiveness for myself that you have for me. I no
longer want to be my own worst enemy. Thank you
for being with me on this journey. For strengthening
me and for the courage to continue forward. I have
control over my emotions, they don't control me. I
am free indeed. It is done and so, Amen.

Day Two

RELEASE AFFIRMATION

I release depression, anxiety, and unworthiness.

POSITIVE AFFIRMATION

I am doing the best I can. God loves me and
I am precious and valuable in God's sight.

SCRIPTURE STUDY

"Since you are precious in my sight,
since you are honored and I love you,
I will give other men in your place..."
–Isaiah 43:4, NIV

DAILY PRAYER

God, thank you for this time of growth and healing.
Help me to have the same compassion and
forgiveness for myself that you have for me. I no
longer want to be my own worst enemy. Thank you
for being with me on this journey. For strengthening
me and for the courage to continue forward. I have
control over my emotions, they don't control me. I
am free indeed. It is done and so, Amen.

Day Three

RELEASE AFFIRMATION

I release the need to reject myself or
feel rejected by others.

POSITIVE AFFIRMATION

I am worthy of my own love and acceptance.

SCRIPTURE STUDY

*"For God has not given us a spirit of fear and
timidity, but of power, love, and self-discipline."*
–2 Timothy 1:7, NLT

DAILY PRAYER

God, thank you for this time of growth and healing.
Help me to have the same compassion and
forgiveness for myself that you have for me. I no
longer want to be my own worst enemy. Thank you
for being with me on this journey. For strengthening
me and for the courage to continue forward. I have
control over my emotions, they don't control me. I
am free indeed. It is done and so, Amen.

Day Four

RELEASE AFFIRMATION

I release the need to feel and be unworthy.

POSITIVE AFFIRMATION

I am worthy and deserving of good in my life.

SCRIPTURE STUDY

*"I pray that out of his glorious riches he may
strengthen you with power through his
Spirit in your inner being."*

–Ephesians 3:16, NIV

DAILY PRAYER

God, thank you for this time of growth and healing.
Help me to have the same compassion and
forgiveness for myself that you have for me. I no
longer want to be my own worst enemy. Thank you
for being with me on this journey. For strengthening
me and for the courage to continue forward. I have
control over my emotions, they don't control me. I
am free indeed. It is done and so, Amen

RELEASE AFFIRMATION

I release the need to be a people pleaser.

POSITIVE AFFIRMATION

I validate and accept myself just as I am.

SCRIPTURE STUDY

*"Our purpose is to please God, not people.
God alone examines the motives of our hearts."*
–Thessalonians 2:4, NLT

DAILY PRAYER

God, thank you for this time of growth and healing.
Help me to have the same compassion and
forgiveness for myself that you have for me. I no
longer want to be my own worst enemy. Thank you
for being with me on this journey. For strengthening
me and for the courage to continue forward. I have
control over my emotions, they don't control me. I
am free indeed. It is done and so, Amen

RELEASE AFFIRMATION

I release the need to create suffering in my life.

POSITIVE AFFIRMATION

I forgive myself and let go of the past. In every moment I have the power to be happy by choice.

SCRIPTURE STUDY

"Let the godly rejoice. Let them be glad in God's presence. Let them be filled with joy."
–Psalm 68:3, NLT

DAILY PRAYER

God, thank you for this time of growth and healing. Help me to have the same compassion and forgiveness for myself that you have for me. I no longer want to be my own worst enemy. Thank you for being with me on this journey. For strengthening me and for the courage to continue forward. I have control over my emotions, they don't control me. I am free indeed. It is done and so, Amen

RELEASE AFFIRMATION

I release low self-esteem and low self-worth.

POSITIVE AFFIRMATION

I am powerful, confident, and secure in who I am.

SCRIPTURE STUDY

*"For the LORD will be your confidence And will
keep your foot from being caught."*
–Proverbs 3:26

DAILY PRAYER

God, thank you for this time of growth and healing.
Help me to have the same compassion and
forgiveness for myself that you have for me. I no
longer want to be my own worst enemy. Thank you
for being with me on this journey. For strengthening
me and for the courage to continue forward. I have
control over my emotions, they don't control me. I
am free indeed. It is done and so, Amen

Week One Reflection

_____

_____

_____

_____

_____

_____

_____

_____

_____

_____

_____

_____

_____

_____

_____

_____

_____

_____

Week Two Reflection

Week Three Reflection

Week Four Reflection

_____

_____

_____

_____

_____

_____

_____

_____

_____

_____

_____

_____

_____

_____

_____

_____

_____

Week Five Reflection

_____

_____

_____

_____

_____

_____

_____

_____

_____

_____

_____

_____

_____

_____

_____

_____

_____

_____

_____

PART III

Healing
YOUR
Body

Day One

RELEASE AFFIRMATION

I release any sickness and disease that has
taken residence in my body.

POSITIVE AFFIRMATION

I am healed and whole, mind, body, and spirit.

SCRIPTURE STUDY

*"But he was pierced for our rebellion, crushed for
our sins. He was beaten so we could be whole.
He was whipped so we could be healed."*
–Isaiah 53:5, NLT

DAILY PRAYER

God, thank you that there is no sickness in the
kingdom. Thank you that you are everything
I need. Everything I need for my complete healing
can be found in you. By your stripes I am healed,
whole, and restored. I repent and turn from the
ways I've gone that are opposite of what was
best for me. It is done and so, Amen.

Day Two

RELEASE AFFIRMATION

I release barriers in my mind and life that are
keeping me away from optimal health.

POSITIVE AFFIRMATION

My body is healthy, thriving, and energetic.

SCRIPTURE STUDY

*"O Lord, if you heal me, I will be truly healed;
if you save me, I will be truly saved.
My praises are for you alone!"*
–Jeremiah 17:14, NLT

DAILY PRAYER

God, thank you that there is no sickness in the
kingdom. Thank you that you are everything
I need. Everything I need for my complete healing
can be found in you. By your stripes I am healed,
whole, and restored. I repent and turn from the
ways I've gone that are opposite of what was
best for me. It is done and so, Amen.

Day Three

RELEASE AFFIRMATION

I release the need to create sickness and
disease in my body.

POSITIVE AFFIRMATION

I give myself permission to heal inside and out.

SCRIPTURE STUDY

*"Everyone tried to touch him, because healing
power went out from him, and he healed everyone."*
–Luke 6:19, NLT

DAILY PRAYER

God, thank you that there is no sickness in the
kingdom. Thank you that you are everything
I need. Everything I need for my complete healing
can be found in you. By your stripes I am healed,
whole, and restored. I repent and turn from the
ways I've gone that are opposite of what was
best for me. It is done and so, Amen.

RELEASE AFFIRMATION

I release every habit that doesn't serve me.

POSITIVE AFFIRMATION

I am patient with myself on my journey
to better physical health.

SCRIPTURE STUDY

*"'I will give you back your health and
heal your wounds,' says the Lord."*
–Jeremiah 30:17, NLT

DAILY PRAYER

God, thank you that there is no sickness in the
kingdom. Thank you that you are everything
I need. Everything I need for my complete healing
can be found in you. By your stripes I am healed,
whole, and restored. I repent and turn from the
ways I've gone that are opposite of what was
best for me. It is done and so, Amen.

Day Five

RELEASE AFFIRMATION

I release the need to idolize fake depictions
of health and wellness.

POSITIVE AFFIRMATION

I am comfortable in my own skin and working
toward the best version of myself.

SCRIPTURE STUDY

*"You are precious and honored in my sight,
and I love you."*
–Isaiah 43:4, NIV

DAILY PRAYER

God, thank you that there is no sickness in the
kingdom. Thank you that you are everything
I need. Everything I need for my complete healing
can be found in you. By your stripes I am healed,
whole, and restored. I repent and turn from the
ways I've gone that are opposite of what was
best for me. It is done and so, Amen.

Day Six

RELEASE AFFIRMATION
I release the need to abuse my body.

POSITIVE AFFIRMATION
I am God's masterpiece. I am thankful for my body
and I will take better care of God's gift to me.

SCRIPTURE STUDY

"For we are God's workmanship, created in
Christ Jesus to do good works,
which God created in advance for us to do."
–Ephesians 2:10, NIV

DAILY PRAYER

God, thank you that there is no sickness in the
kingdom. Thank you that you are everything
I need. Everything I need for my complete healing
can be found in you. By your stripes I am healed,
whole, and restored. I repent and turn from the
ways I've gone that are opposite of what was
best for me. It is done and so, Amen.

RELEASE AFFIRMATION

I release the need to conform to
other's ideals of beauty.

POSITIVE AFFIRMATION

I am happy with myself and the way I look.

SCRIPTURE STUDY

*"As water reflects a face,
so a man's heart reflects the man."*
–Proverbs 27:19, NIV

DAILY PRAYER

God, thank you that there is no sickness in the
kingdom. Thank you that you are everything
I need. Everything I need for my complete healing
can be found in you. By your stripes I am healed,
whole, and restored. I repent and turn from the
ways I've gone that are opposite of what was
best for me. It is done and so, Amen.

Week One Reflection

_____

_____

_____

_____

_____

_____

_____

_____

_____

_____

_____

_____

_____

_____

_____

_____

_____

_____

Week Two Reflection

_____

_____

_____

_____

_____

_____

_____

_____

_____

_____

_____

_____

_____

_____

_____

_____

_____

Week Three Reflection

Week Four Reflection

_____

_____

_____

_____

_____

_____

_____

_____

_____

_____

_____

_____

_____

_____

_____

_____

_____

_____

Week Five Reflection

_____

_____

_____

_____

_____

_____

_____

_____

_____

_____

_____

_____

_____

_____

_____

_____

_____

_____

_____

PART IV

Healing

YOUR

Relationships

Day One

RELEASE AFFIRMATION

I release the need to feel like a victim in life
and in my relationships.

POSITIVE AFFIRMATION

I take responsibility for and have control over my
thoughts, actions, and reactions.

SCRIPTURE STUDY

*"Each one should test their own actions. Then they
can take pride in themselves alone, without
comparing themselves to others."*
–Galatians 6:4, NIV

DAILY PRAYER

God, thank you for the revelation that the most
important relationships I can improve is with
myself and with you. Thank you for the gift of
self-awareness, which is changing my life and my
other relationships for the better. I am healthy and
so are my relationships. It is done and so, Amen.

Day Two

RELEASE AFFIRMATION

I release the need to hold on to
toxic relationships and people.

POSITIVE AFFIRMATION

I am in balanced and healthy relationships, giving
and receiving love, effortlessly and unconditionally.

SCRIPTURE STUDY

*"There are 'friends' who destroy each other, but a
real friend sticks closer than a brother."*
–Proverbs 18:24, NLT

DAILY PRAYER

God, thank you for the revelation that the most
important relationships I can improve is with
myself and with you. Thank you for the gift of
self-awareness, which is changing my life and my
other relationships for the better. I am healthy and
so are my relationships. It is done and so, Amen.

RELEASE AFFIRMATION

I release the need to hold grudges
and harbor unforgiveness.

POSITIVE AFFIRMATION

I am extending forgiveness to myself and others.

SCRIPTURE STUDY

*"Do not bear a grudge against others, but settle
your differences with them, so that you will not
commit a sin because of them."*
–Leviticus 19:17-18, NIV

DAILY PRAYER

God, thank you for the revelation that the most
important relationships I can improve is with
myself and with you. Thank you for the gift of
self-awareness, which is changing my life and my
other relationships for the better. I am healthy and
so are my relationships. It is done and so, Amen.

Day Four

RELEASE AFFIRMATION

I release the need for validation from others.

POSITIVE AFFIRMATION

I am enough. My opinion of myself and
God's are the only two that matter in my life.

SCRIPTURE STUDY

*"The crucible for silver, the furnace for gold, but
man is tested by the praise he receives."*
–Proverbs 27:21, NIV

DAILY PRAYER

God, thank you for the revelation that the most
important relationships I can improve is with
myself and with you. Thank you for the gift of
self-awareness, which is changing my life and my
other relationships for the better. I am healthy and
so are my relationships. It is done and so, Amen.

Day Five

RELEASE AFFIRMATION

I release bitterness, resentment, and anger towards
people who have hurt me in the past.

POSITIVE AFFIRMATION

I am free to live a happy and peaceful life.

SCRIPTURE STUDY

*"Make allowance for each other's faults.
Forgive anyone who offends you.
Remember, the Lord forgave you..."*
–Colossians 3:13, NLT

DAILY PRAYER

God, thank you for the revelation that the most
important relationships I can improve is with
myself and with you. Thank you for the gift of
self-awareness, which is changing my life and my
other relationships for the better. I am healthy and
so are my relationships. It is done and so, Amen.

RELEASE AFFIRMATION

I release the need to blame others for the
results I am getting in my life.

POSITIVE AFFIRMATION

I take full responsibility for
my life and my own happiness.

SCRIPTURE STUDY

*"Don't be misled—you cannot mock the justice of
God. You will always harvest what you plant."*
–Galatians 6:7, NLT

DAILY PRAYER

God, thank you for the revelation that the most
important relationships I can improve is with
myself and with you. Thank you for the gift of
self-awareness, which is changing my life and my
other relationships for the better. I am healthy and
so are my relationships. It is done and so, Amen.

Day Seven

RELEASE AFFIRMATION

I release the need to control others.

POSITIVE AFFIRMATION

I am willing to extend to others
the love and grace God gives me.

SCRIPTURE STUDY

*"'My grace is all you need. My power works
best in weakness.' So now I am glad to boast
about my weaknesses, so that the power of
Christ can work through me."*
–I Corinthians 12:9, NLT

DAILY PRAYER

God, thank you for the revelation that the most
important relationships I can improve is with
myself and with you. Thank you for the gift of
self-awareness, which is changing my life and my
other relationships for the better. I am healthy and
so are my relationships. It is done and so, Amen.

Week One Reflection

_____

_____

_____

_____

_____

_____

_____

_____

_____

_____

_____

_____

_____

_____

_____

_____

_____

_____

Week Two Reflection

_____

_____

_____

_____

_____

_____

_____

_____

_____

_____

_____

_____

_____

_____

_____

_____

_____

_____

Week Three Reflection

_____

_____

_____

_____

_____

_____

_____

_____

_____

_____

_____

_____

_____

_____

_____

_____

_____

Week Four Reflection

Week Five Reflection

PART V

Healing YOUR Dreams

Day One

RELEASE AFFIRMATION

I release the habit of silencing my inner child.

POSITIVE AFFIRMATION

I accept and embrace the guidance of my inner child. It guides me toward my true purpose.

SCRIPTURE STUDY

"For I know the plans I have for you,"
says the Lord. "They are plans for good and not
for disaster, to give you a future and a hope."
–Jeremiah 29:11, NLT

DAILY PRAYER

God, thank you for blessing me with my unique gifts, talents, and abilities. You created me to be unique and purposeful in my living and career. I pray that you'll rekindle the passion for my dreams. I am not a victim. I am a victor and it's not too late for me or my dreams to be realized. It is done and so, Amen.

Day Two

RELEASE AFFIRMATION

I release the need to suppress my talents and gifts.

POSITIVE AFFIRMATION

I am gifted and talented. God created me for
and with a divine purpose.

SCRIPTURE STUDY

*"I have filled him with the Spirit of God,
giving him great wisdom, ability, and
expertise in all kinds of crafts."*
–Exodus 31:3, NLT

DAILY PRAYER

God, thank you for blessing me with my unique
gifts, talents, and abilities. You created me to be
unique and purposeful in my living and career.
I pray that you'll rekindle the passion for my
dreams. I am not a victim. I am a victor and
it's not too late for me or my dreams to be
realized. It is done and so, Amen.

RELEASE AFFIRMATION

I release the need to live out
other people's expectations of me.

POSITIVE AFFIRMATION

I embrace my unique path and purpose for living.

SCRIPTURE STUDY

*"Each of you should use whatever gift you have
received to serve others, as faithful stewards of
God's grace in its various forms."*
–I Peter 4:10, NIV

DAILY PRAYER

God, thank you for blessing me with my unique
gifts, talents, and abilities. You created me to be
unique and purposeful in my living and career.
I pray that you'll rekindle the passion for my
dreams. I am not a victim. I am a victor and
it's not too late for me or my dreams to be
realized. It is done and so, Amen.

Day Four

RELEASE AFFIRMATION

I release the need to diminish my dreams and goals.

POSITIVE AFFIRMATION

I give myself permission to follow my dreams and reach my goals. The bigger, the better the blessings.

SCRIPTURE STUDY

"For I can do everything through Christ who gives me strength."
–Philippians 4:13, NLT

DAILY PRAYER

God, thank you for blessing me with my unique gifts, talents, and abilities. You created me to be unique and purposeful in my living and career. I pray that you'll rekindle the passion for my dreams. I am not a victim. I am a victor and it's not too late for me or my dreams to be realized. It is done and so, Amen.

Day Five

RELEASE AFFIRMATION

I release the need to limit myself and my thoughts around what's possible for my life.

POSITIVE AFFIRMATION

I am unlimited potential.
I will realize my full potential.

SCRIPTURE STUDY

"Jesus looked at them intently and said, 'Humanly speaking, it is impossible. But with God everything is possible.'"
–Matthew 19:26, NLT

DAILY PRAYER

God, thank you for blessing me with my unique gifts, talents, and abilities. You created me to be unique and purposeful in my living and career. I pray that you'll rekindle the passion for my dreams. I am not a victim. I am a victor and it's not too late for me or my dreams to be realized. It is done and so, Amen.

RELEASE AFFIRMATION

I release the need to make excuses
for why I'm not living my dreams.

POSITIVE AFFIRMATION

I am in control of my actions. At any time I have
the power to change course and live my dreams.

SCRIPTURE STUDY

*"Now faith is being sure of what you hope for and
certain of what you cannot see. Without faith it is
impossible to please God."*
–Hebrews 11:1,6, NIV

DAILY PRAYER

God, thank you for blessing me with my unique
gifts, talents, and abilities. You created me to be
unique and purposeful in my living and career.
I pray that you'll rekindle the passion for my
dreams. I am not a victim. I am a victor and
it's not too late for me or my dreams to be
realized. It is done and so, Amen.

Day Seven

RELEASE AFFIRMATION

I release the fear attached to inaction that's
keeping me from taking steps toward my dreams.

POSITIVE AFFIRMATION

I have the courage, strength, and ability to make
my dreams come true. It's possible for me too.

SCRIPTURE STUDY

*"This is my command—be strong and courageous!
Do not be afraid or discouraged. For the Lord your
God is with you wherever you go."*
–Joshua 1:9, NLT

DAILY PRAYER

God, thank you for blessing me with my unique
gifts, talents, and abilities. You created me to be
unique and purposeful in my living and career.
I pray that you'll rekindle the passion for my
dreams. I am not a victim. I am a victor and
it's not too late for me or my dreams to be
realized. It is done and so, Amen.

Week One Reflection

_____

_____

_____

_____

_____

_____

_____

_____

_____

_____

_____

_____

_____

_____

_____

_____

_____

Week Two Reflection

Week Three Reflection

_____

_____

_____

_____

_____

_____

_____

_____

_____

_____

_____

_____

_____

_____

_____

_____

_____

Week Four Reflection

_____

_____

_____

_____

_____

_____

_____

_____

_____

_____

_____

_____

_____

_____

_____

_____

_____

_____

Week Five Reflection

_____

_____

_____

_____

_____

_____

_____

_____

_____

_____

_____

_____

_____

_____

_____

_____

_____

_____

PART VI

Healing

YOUR

Finances

Day One

RELEASE AFFIRMATION

I release the habit of operating from a place
of lack and scarcity in my life.

POSITIVE AFFIRMATION

I've been given the ability to create wealth and
live a life full of abundance and
prosperity. I will prosper.

SCRIPTURE STUDY

*"But remember the Lord your God, for it is he who
gives you the ability to produce wealth..."*
–Deuteronomy 8:18, NIV

DAILY PRAYER

God, thank you for giving me the ability to create
wealth. Help me to release wrong thinking around
money and success. I am worthy of abundance and
prosperity. I choose to live life more abundantly
starting today. I understand it is my choice. I will
speak your divine power over my finances and am
open to divine increase. It is done and so, Amen.

Day Two

RELEASE AFFIRMATION

I release any trace of poverty mentality and lack
from my conscious and subconscious mind.

POSITIVE AFFIRMATION

I am prosperous and thriving
in every area of my life.

SCRIPTURE STUDY

*"The Lord your God will bless you as he has
promised. You will lend money to many
nations but will never need to borrow."*
–Deuteronomy 15:6, NLT

DAILY PRAYER

God, thank you for giving me the ability to create
wealth. Help me to release wrong thinking around
money and success. I am worthy of abundance and
prosperity. I choose to live life more abundantly
starting today. I understand it is my choice. I will
speak your divine power over my finances and am
open to divine increase. It is done and so, Amen.

Day Three

RELEASE AFFIRMATION

I release old, outdated beliefs about money.
My background doesn't determine my future.

POSITIVE AFFIRMATION

I am worthy and actively preparing for the
blessings God has for me. God wants to bless me.

SCRIPTURE STUDY

*"I want you to realize what a rich and glorious
inheritance God has given his people."*
–Ephesians 1:18, NLT

DAILY PRAYER

God, thank you for giving me the ability to create
wealth. Help me to release wrong thinking around
money and success. I am worthy of abundance and
prosperity. I choose to live life more abundantly
starting today. I understand it is my choice. I will
speak your divine power over my finances and am
open to divine increase. It is done and so, Amen.

Day Four

RELEASE AFFIRMATION

I release any feelings of unworthiness
related to money and wealth.

POSITIVE AFFIRMATION

I am worthy of success and wealth.
There is enough for me too.

SCRIPTURE STUDY

*"The blessing of the Lord makes one rich,
and He adds no sorrow with it."*
–Proverbs 10:22, NLT

DAILY PRAYER

God, thank you for giving me the ability to create
wealth. Help me to release wrong thinking around
money and success. I am worthy of abundance and
prosperity. I choose to live life more abundantly
starting today. I understand it is my choice. I will
speak your divine power over my finances and am
open to divine increase. It is done and so, Amen.

Day Five

RELEASE AFFIRMATION

I release the need to continue to play small out of
fear or because I won't believe God for more.

POSITIVE AFFIRMATION

I deserve to experience the blessings of God in
mind, body, spirit, and material wealth.

SCRIPTURE STUDY

"The Lord is my shepherd; I lack nothing."
–Psalm 23:1, NIV

DAILY PRAYER

God, thank you for giving me the ability to create
wealth. Help me to release wrong thinking around
money and success. I am worthy of abundance and
prosperity. I choose to live life more abundantly
starting today. I understand it is my choice. I will
speak your divine power over my finances and am
open to divine increase. It is done and so, Amen.

Day Six

RELEASE AFFIRMATION

I release the need to complain and speak negatively about my finances, career, and money in general.

POSITIVE AFFIRMATION

I am grateful for everything I have. Gratitude opens up the doors for God to bless me with more.

SCRIPTURE STUDY

"Let them shout for joy and be glad…
Let the Lord be magnified,
Who has pleasure in the prosperity of His servant."
–Psalm 35:27

DAILY PRAYER

God, thank you for giving me the ability to create wealth. Help me to release wrong thinking around money and success. I am worthy of abundance and prosperity. I choose to live life more abundantly starting today. I understand it is my choice. I will speak your divine power over my finances and am open to divine increase. It is done and so, Amen.

RELEASE AFFIRMATION

I release the need to worry about money and
operate in fear around my finances.

POSITIVE AFFIRMATION

I trust God to supply my needs and teach me how
to manage the wealth in store for me as I seek Him.

SCRIPTURE STUDY

*"Don't worry about anything; instead,
pray about everything. Tell God what you need
and thank him for all he has done."*
–Philippians 4:6, NLT

DAILY PRAYER

God, thank you for giving me the ability to create
wealth. Help me to release wrong thinking around
money and success. I am worthy of abundance and
prosperity. I choose to live life more abundantly
starting today. I understand it is my choice. I will
speak your divine power over my finances and am
open to divine increase. It is done and so, Amen.

Week One Reflection

_____

_____

_____

_____

_____

_____

_____

_____

_____

_____

_____

_____

_____

_____

_____

_____

_____

_____

Week Two Reflection

_____

_____

_____

_____

_____

_____

_____

_____

_____

_____

_____

_____

_____

_____

_____

_____

Week Three Reflection

Week Four Reflection

Week Five Reflection

PART VII

Healing

YOUR

Spirituality

Day One

RELEASE AFFIRMATION

I release the need to gossip about
my problems or others.

POSITIVE AFFIRMATION

I am committing to daily prayer to
strengthen my relationship with God.

SCRIPTURE STUDY

*"I pour out all my complaints before God and tell
him all my troubles. For I am overwhelmed."*
–Psalm 142:2-3, NLT

DAILY PRAYER

God, thank you for the grace and power to change
everything about my life that doesn't line up with
your divine will for me. I seek your divine guidance
on changing my daily habits to manifest everything
I need to live life more abundantly. Abundance is
my birthright. It is done and so, Amen.

Day Two

RELEASE AFFIRMATION

I release any anger and resentment
I have toward God and the church.

POSITIVE AFFIRMATION

I am drawing nearer to God and
God in return is drawing nearer to me.

SCRIPTURE STUDY

*"Come close to God, and
God will come close to you."*
–James 4:8, NLT

DAILY PRAYER

God, thank you for the grace and power to change
everything about my life that doesn't line up with
your divine will for me. I seek your divine guidance
on changing my daily habits to manifest everything
I need to live life more abundantly. Abundance is
my birthright. It is done and so, Amen.

Day Three

RELEASE AFFIRMATION

I release the need to operate from a
place of fear and uncertainty.

POSITIVE AFFIRMATION

I am powerful, confident, and
successful in all of my ventures.

SCRIPTURE STUDY

*"This is my command—be strong and courageous!
Do not be afraid or discouraged. For the Lord your
God is with you wherever you go."*
–Joshua 1:9, NLT

DAILY PRAYER

God, thank you for the grace and power to change
everything about my life that doesn't line up with
your divine will for me. I seek your divine guidance
on changing my daily habits to manifest everything
I need to live life more abundantly. Abundance is
my birthright. It is done and so, Amen.

RELEASE AFFIRMATION

I release the need to put God in a box.

POSITIVE AFFIRMATION

I am open to allowing God to be God in my body, mind, emotions, relationships, and finances.

SCRIPTURE STUDY

"Now to him who is able to do immeasurably more than all we ask or imagine, according to his power that is at work within us."

–Ephesians 3:20, NIV

DAILY PRAYER

God, thank you for the grace and power to change everything about my life that doesn't line up with your divine will for me. I seek your divine guidance on changing my daily habits to manifest everything I need to live life more abundantly. Abundance is my birthright. It is done and so, Amen.

RELEASE AFFIRMATION

I release the need to depend on
myself for everything.

POSITIVE AFFIRMATION

I am seeking God's will for my life.

SCRIPTURE STUDY

*"Trust in the Lord with all your heart and
lean not on your own understanding."*
–Proverbs 3:5, NIV

DAILY PRAYER

God, thank you for the grace and power to change
everything about my life that doesn't line up with
your divine will for me. I seek your divine guidance
on changing my daily habits to manifest everything
I need to live life more abundantly. Abundance is
my birthright. It is done and so, Amen.

RELEASE AFFIRMATION

I release the need to put others in God's place.

POSITIVE AFFIRMATION

I am allowing God to reign freely in my life,
and I trust God completely.

SCRIPTURE STUDY

*"Do not put your trust in princes, in human beings,
who cannot save. Blessed are those whose help is the
God of Jacob; whose hope is in the Lord their God."*
–Psalm 146:3,5, NIV

DAILY PRAYER

God, thank you for the grace and power to change
everything about my life that doesn't line up with
your divine will for me. I seek your divine guidance
on changing my daily habits to manifest everything
I need to live life more abundantly. Abundance is
my birthright. It is done and so, Amen.

Day Seven

RELEASE AFFIRMATION

I release the need to judge myself or others.

POSITIVE AFFIRMATION

I am doing the best I can and so is everyone else
according to their knowledge and abilities.

SCRIPTURE STUDY

"Since you are precious in my sight,
since you are honored and I love you,
I will give other men in your place..."
–Isaiah 43:4, NIV

DAILY PRAYER

God, thank you for the grace and power to change
everything about my life that doesn't line up with
your divine will for me. I seek your divine guidance
on changing my daily habits to manifest everything
I need to live life more abundantly. Abundance is
my birthright. It is done and so, Amen.

Week One Reflection

_____

_____

_____

_____

_____

_____

_____

_____

_____

_____

_____

_____

_____

_____

_____

_____

_____

_____

Week Two Reflection

_____

_____

_____

_____

_____

_____

_____

_____

_____

_____

_____

_____

_____

_____

_____

_____

_____

Week Three Reflection

Week Four Reflection

_____

_____

_____

_____

_____

_____

_____

_____

_____

_____

_____

_____

_____

_____

_____

_____

_____

Week Five Reflection

_____

_____

_____

_____

_____

_____

_____

_____

_____

_____

_____

_____

_____

_____

_____

_____

_____

_____

_____

*"Beloved, I pray that you may prosper
in all things and be in health,
just as your soul prospers."*
–3 John 2:2

Author Disclaimer

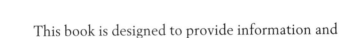

This book is designed to provide information and motivation to readers.

Neither the publisher nor author shall be liable for any physical, psychological, emotional, financial, or commercial damages, including, but not limited to, special, incidental, consequential or other damages.

Every person is different, and the advice and strategies contained herein may not be suitable for your situation. Our views and rights are the same: You are responsible for your own choices, actions, and results.

About the Author

Stephan Labossiere is *the* "Relationship Guy." An authority on real love, real talk, real relationships. The brand *Stephan Speaks* is synonymous with happier relationships and healthier people around the globe. For more than a decade, Stephan has committed himself to breaking down relationship barriers, pushing past common facades, and exposing the truth. It is his understanding of REAL relationships that has empowered millions of people, clients and readers alike, to create their best lives by being able to experience and sustain greater love.

Seen, heard, and chronicled in national and international media outlets including; the *Tom Joyner Morning Show, The Examiner, ABC, GQ,* and *Huffington Post Live.* The certified life & relationship coach, speaker, and award winning, bestselling author is the voice that the world tunes into for answers to their difficult relationship woes. From understanding the opposite sex, to navigating the paths and avoiding the pitfalls of relationships and self-growth, Stephan's relationship advice and insight helps countless men and women overcome the situations hindering them from achieving an authentically amazing life.

Stephan is highly sought-after because he is able to dispel the myths of relationship breakdowns and obstacles–platonic, romantic, and otherwise—with fervor and finesse. His signature style, relatability, and passion make international audiences sit up and pay attention.

"My message is simple: life and relationships require truth. The willingness to speak truth and the bravery to acknowledge truth is paramount."

Are you listening?

Enough said.

JUST RELEASED BY
Stephan Speaks

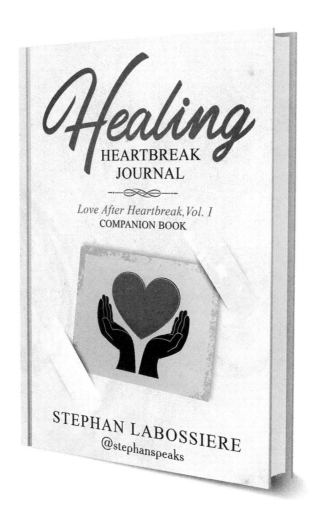

www.HealingHeartbreakBook.com

www.LoveAfterHeartbreak.com

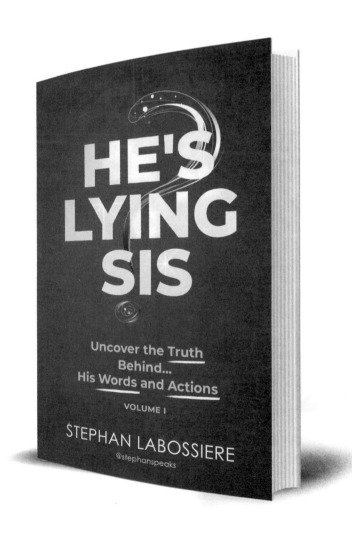

www.HesLyingSis.com

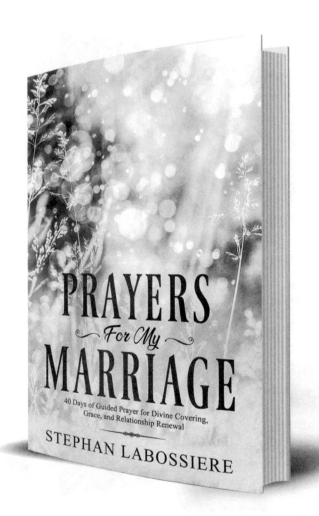

www.PrayersForMyMarriageBook.com

POPULAR BOOKS BY
Stephan Speaks

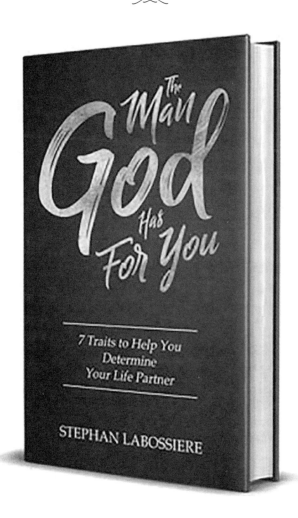

www.TheManGodHasForMe.com

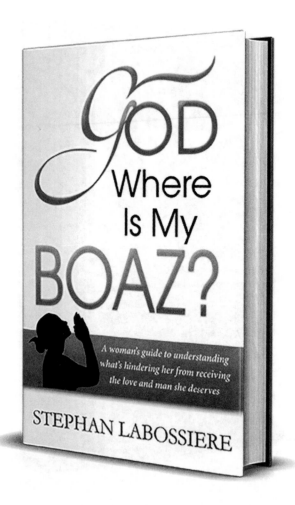

www.GodWhereIsMyBoaz.com

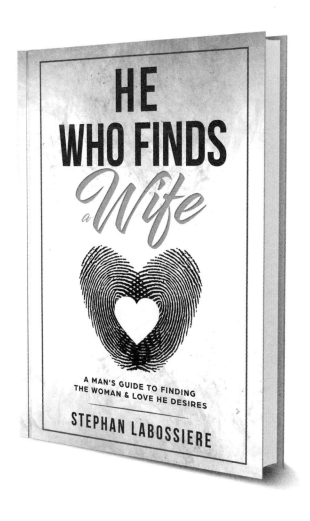

www.HeWhoFinds.com

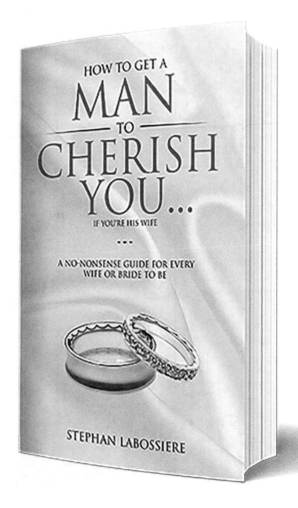

www.GetAManToCherishYou.com

www.BetterMarriageBetterLoving.com

A JOY TO WORK WITH

As someone who has studied the role of men and women in relationships in our society for many years, it has been a joy to get to know and work with Stephan. His knowledge and candid from the heart writings and speaking on the topic of relationships are a breath of fresh air and sure to take you and your relationships to a more authentic and loving way of being.

—Tom Preston

More relationship resources can be found at
www.StephanSpeaks.com/shop/

You can also follow me on
Twitter & Instagram: **@StephanSpeaks**
or find me on Facebook under
"Stephan Speaks Relationships"